WHAT
WOMEN
SHOULD
UNDERSTAND
ABOUT
MEN

Nancy Van Pelt

First published 2009
Reprinted 2019

© 2009

All rights reserved. No part of this publication
may be reproduced in any form without prior
permission from the publisher.

British Library Cataloguing in Publication Data.

A catalogue record for this book is available from
the British Library.

ISBN 978-1-906381-50-9

Published by Autumn House, Grantham, Lincolnshire.

Printed in India.

Too tired for sex?

Sexual desire is different from sexual arousal. Arousal occurs when the body has been stimulated. Sexual desire shows up in our sex drive or libido.

Sexual energy can be absorbed on other projects – establishing a new business, caring for a new baby, sports, managing several school-age children.

For those who live complicated, busy lives, there may never be enough time or energy to feel sexual desire. To correct this, clear away distractions. The first and easiest thing to do is to turn off the TV. Spend quiet moments together. . . .

Children can be a distraction, particularly for mothers of preschoolers. A child with health or behavioural problems can consume so much energy that parents find themselves having little sexual interest in each other. Such couples need time away without the children.

Sexual fulfilment is more likely to happen when we know ourselves and one another intimately, behave lovingly towards one another, are both trustworthy and trusting, and anticipate and plan for sexual times. . . .

'Not tonight, dear!'

A couple arrive home after a night on the town. She is sitting at her dressing table, getting ready for bed. He places two aspirins and a glass of water in front of her. She asks, 'What's that for?' 'Your headache,' he says. 'But I don't have a headache!' 'Gotcha!'

Frequency of sexual encounters between couples depends on a number of factors such as age, health, social and business pressures, emotional readiness, an ability to communicate about sex, and many other variables.

Most men think about sex more often, are more easily aroused and want to have sex more frequently than their partners do. Researchers tell us that men and women have the same half dozen sex hormones. Fact is that men have ten to twenty times more testosterone than women. That explains a great deal.

A sexually satisfied man is an easier man to live with than one who is not.

Most men do not fully appreciate or understand the complexity of a woman's sexuality.

The first sign of
arousal in the man is
an erection. This occurs
within a few seconds
after an erotic thought,
a stimulating sight or
a caress.

Some couples think that the main goal in intercourse is to reach orgasm simultaneously. Since only about 17% of all couples experience a simultaneous orgasm – and even then only on occasion – this leaves many couples wondering whether their sexual experiences are lacking.

Trying to achieve
orgasm at the
same time
can actually
make sex less
fulfilling. . . .

When a couple achieves orgasm together, each is so absorbed with their own intense pleasure that all attention is concentrated on self. One minute she enjoys the full extent of his attention; the next minute he is absorbed in himself. In the same way, he will miss experiencing the full extent of her pleasure. . . .

Four practices can increase the intensity of pleasure for the male:

1. Waiting twenty-four hours after the previous orgasm.

2. Lengthening foreplay and excitement.

3. Increasing the imagination by seeing and feeling the wife's ecstatic response to his skilful stimulation.

4. Contracting the anal sphincter muscles during orgasm.

These can ruin your sex life

Illness, drugs, anger, performance anxieties, shame, guilt.

Does your husband experience premature ejaculation?

It is curable. Read pages 206-208 of my *HIGHLY EFFECTIVE MARRIAGE* and find out how.

Don't let him call you 'frigid'. Research has proved that all married women are capable of achieving orgasm. 'Pre-orgasmic' is more appropriate, since orgasm for females is a learned experience.

A woman's orgasmic response is closely connected to her feelings about herself. Resentment, bitterness, misinformation, and tired attitudes build sexual barriers for a woman that make it difficult for her to respond to her husband.

Your most important sex organ is the brain. It must say, 'OK, go ahead' for you to be sexually satisfied.

Let's talk about it

Why is it that the most
fascinating subject known
to humankind is the most
difficult for a couple to talk
about?

Unless you do talk about it,
you will revert to childish
ways of sending indirect
messages.

When a sexual problem is not addressed, it does anything but disappear. It tends to grow in its dimension and impact. Communication on sexual preferences produces a happier sex life.

Does sexual desire decline with age? Sex invariably changes, but that doesn't mean it dies. Women in their twenties are the least likely to achieve orgasm, while those in their forties are the likeliest.

Women in their thirties start taking more sexual initiative. These women feel a marked increase in the need for orgasm.

It is one thing to have knowledge about why and how your partner responds differently and another thing to accept the differences and change your behaviour accordingly. To a large degree, a woman can make a husband feel either great about himself sexually or inadequate.

Making love should not be a one-way street with only the husband satisfying the wife. He needs and wants a partner who knows how to make love to him.

Make him feel sexually attractive

A man needs to know his mate finds him sexually attractive before he can respond to her emotional needs.

Understand what turns him on

The glimpse of you in
a breezy nightie may
be all it takes to flip his
switch. But make sure
that he knows that you
admire him physically.

God created the male to be sexually responsive to external stimuli. His genitals are on the outside, and so is his sexuality.

Romance him with touch

A man usually wants direct and immediate genital stimulation.

Extend lovemaking

If a man has had
fifteen to twenty
minutes of stimulation
prior to intercourse,
it will provide greater
intensity.

Feel good about yourself and your body

If you don't think of yourself as sexy, you won't be sexy. You don't have to be a beauty queen, but you must feel good about your body.

Do what you need to
do to help yourself feel
attractive. Exercise. Wear
the clothes that make you
(and him) feel sexy. Pamper
yourself in the bath. Enjoy
the oils, lotion, facials that
give you confidence about
your attractiveness and
bedroom appeal.

Make sex a priority

Nothing stymies a
woman's interest in
sex more than fatigue.
A loving wife will sort
out priorities so that
sex doesn't languish
in last place.

One of the key factors in achieving a great sex life is remaining committed to one partner. It's called fidelity. Confining sex exclusively to one's partner for a lifetime is the only way to build an emotionally healthy, stable relationship.

Choosing to restrict one's sexual focus to a lifetime partner is basic to character building. Your character defines who you are.

Self-control is a key ingredient in all sexual expression. Without it, not only does society disintegrate, but a person becomes unpredictable and dangerous.

Husbands and wives should aim to be imaginative, creative and willing lovers. God designed that sex (unhampered by selfishness) be exciting, enjoyable and fulfilling.

No man is entirely immune from ego problems. Today's highly competitive, complex society continuously subjects men to major assaults on their masculinity. A man's ego is far more vulnerable than a woman's.

The strength of the male ego greatly affects the health of the marital relationship. The man with a healthy self-image and a strong sense of his worth and masculinity is far happier and more competent in coping with life than the male plagued by doubts and feelings of inadequacy.

A male ego is like
walking a tightrope
over an abyss of
possible failure every
day. Men live an inch
from losing all the
time. Today's society
sets a high standard
for its men.

Today's world expects a man to be a sensitive husband, a good lover to his wife, an involved father, the life and soul of every party, and excel in some leisure activity as well. It isn't enough for him to *strive* towards these goals; he must *achieve* them.

Men return home after a hectic day at work in need of balm for their bruised ego. Far too many often find the opposite.

Some women blame their husbands for everything that goes wrong, or undermine them in subtle ways, often without realising it, by complaining about the income they earn. A man's ego suffers when he hears his wife disparaging his earning capacity. . . .

The biggest challenge to the male ego takes place in the bedroom. Today if a man doesn't satisfy his wife every time they make love, he considers himself a failure, even though this goal is unrealistic.

A man may only grunt
when complimented
on his appearance, or
shrug when his golf
game isn't up to par;
but don't think he
doesn't feel these
things deeply. Men
are not meant to cry
or display emotion. . . .

A man will often disguise
feelings of inadequacy
by boasting about his
accomplishments. One
wife was so embarrassed by
this that she put down her
husband publicly, unaware
she'd hit him in his most
vulnerable spot – his
sagging ego.

One of the most vital services a woman can perform for her husband, her marriage and herself, is to fortify her husband's ego when he is under attack.

A wife can take the pressure off him when he is under stress and deal with daily problems quietly by herself. A woman who finds something praiseworthy in her man can help bolster his sagging ego.

A man needs an organised, tranquil home

More than expensive furniture, swimming pools or BMWs in the driveway, men want –. *tranquillity.*

The stress of pleasing a boss, surviving professionally and beating inflation is so severe that a man needs a haven to which he can return. This puts tranquillity at the top of his list of needs.

Who can find tranquillity in the midst of disorganisation, clutter and mess?

If both partners work, they should share chores in the home and responsibility for maintaining its order.

A man appreciates an attractive wife

An attractive wife is one who resembles the woman he married. . . .

If a woman lets her appearance go, her husband will not be stimulated to look at her often. A wife can guard against this by making a reasonable effort to remain attractive.

Casual jeans and a T-shirt look good on a trim woman. Larger women can be attractive, but only when they pay close attention to the cut and lines of their clothing, along with colour and design.

You need not be a startling beauty, but you can do your best with what you have. An attractive woman is not so much born as made. Keep an eye on your 'image'.

A man needs recreational companionship

Girls talk. Boys play. A man wants to enjoy going out and doing things with his wife.

Women join boyfriends/fiancés for activities during dating years.

They need to do it after marriage too.

Women who let opportunities pass to go with their husbands as they pursue leisure-time activities may find that in spite of all their efforts they never build an intimate relationship with their husbands.

Unless a woman learns to adapt and move with her husband into recreational activities, he'll go alone or with his friends. That means the things he enjoys most will never be shared with his wife.

Research confirms that stress is more deadly for men than for women.

For example, twice as many men die from combined heart disease problems than women.

A man needs stress relief

Stress is anything that annoys, threatens, excites, worries, angers, frustrates or challenges self-esteem.

Male stress originates
in four main areas:

1. Body image
2. Career concerns
3. Family concerns
4. The inability to
   share feelings or
   express emotions.

Men tend to release
anger in spurts rather
than in slow-moving
negotiations.

Heated argument
can be hazardous
to a man's health!

While under stress men withdraw and become notoriously quiet. John Gray in *Men Are From Mars and Women Are From Venus* refers to this male reaction as 'going into his cave'.

When a man comes home from a hard day at work, he wants to forget about the pressures and find relief by wrapping the newspaper around himself.

Taking his mind off his problems de-stresses him. Watching TV, going to a football match, working out in the gym. All these can help.

When a man is stressed he often becomes so focused on his stress that he loses awareness of other things. He often becomes distant, forgetful and unresponsive. The larger the problem, the more magnified his absorption by the problem.

At such times it is difficult for the man to give his wife and family the attention they need. The problems and stress hold him in a vice and he is powerless to release himself until he finds a solution.

A woman will find this male tendency easier to live with when she realises that his withdrawal does not mean he doesn't love her. A caring wife will give her husband space during times of stress and problem-solving.

Symptoms of stress include extreme criticism of wife and children; withdrawal from family interaction and conversation; preoccupation; overeating and weight gain; unusual fatigue and tendency to fall asleep; selective deafness – tuning out what he doesn't want to hear.

Reckless driving, a tendency to take chances, an addiction to TV, video or the computer and increased spending – are all increased stress indicators.

One of the best things a woman can do is to encourage her husband to talk about his stress and his feelings. But don't be surprised if he rejects your attempts to help. A man frequently rejects advice from his wife, regardless of how 'right' she may be.

When both partners have the same dominant temperament, both will want to be in charge of everything.

They need to designate in advance who should handle each task.

Love, communication and understanding are all important attributes of a really successful marriage. Yet they may not be enough if the house is in a mess, everyone is hungry, and no one will prepare a meal.

God's original plan
for marriage was for
husband and wife to
live together in perfect
harmony. Before sin
entered, God was the
ultimate leader in the
home.

Many people have misinterpreted the Genesis account of the first marriage. They mistakenly conclude that God designated Adam as the leader of the family. Not in the original play. Eve's role was as 'a helper fit for him' (Genesis 2:18). That made her role no less important than Adam's.

Shouldering different roles does not indicate inferiority or inequality.

God created male and female to complement one another. Just as a successful organisation depends on each employee's ability to assume the position assigned and produce to the best of their ability, so is a marriage interdependent.

Husband and wife are dependent on each other. Although their responsibility and roles differ, they are equal in importance and both are necessary to the well-being of a healthy society.

In several places the Bible says that the husband is the head of the wife. However, notice what is added: 'For the husband is the head of the wife as Christ is the head of the church. . . . Husbands, love your wives, *as Christ loved the church and gave himself up for her.*' (Ephesians 5:23-25, NIV.)

Few men will literally be called upon to die so that their wives can live. So what do these verses mean?

They bring an almost spiritual quality to the position of the husband. Husbands must be to their wives what Christ is to the church.

The overall direction of the entire household falls on the shoulders of the husband. This is literally what the term *husband* means – the male head of the house; one who manages or directs a household.

Under the guise of authoritarian leadership, many men destroy their wives and children. The heavy-handed, commanding, head-of-the-house system has no place in a Christian's life, since it leaves the wife feeling less than an equal partner.

Authoritarian men are usually from authoritarian homes where they have seen such behaviour modelled. Or they may be weak, insecure males who fear letting anyone usurp their authority. In either case, this becomes the only leadership pattern they know.

Behaviours that demonstrate a lack of mutuality may not be violent or physically abusive ones; they may be emotionally abusive ones.

In one study, 53% of a group of couples who were questioned regarding the failure of their marriage said that the downfall was the result of a partner's attempt to control them.

Typical examples of controlling behaviour include making decisions without consulting the other, dictating how the other partner should dress, where they should live, how the money should be spent.

When there is a lack of consideration for the other's wishes, opinions and feelings in the decision-making process – then there's authoritarianism.

When digression from the
authoritarian's agenda
occurs he (or she) makes
immediate attempts to force
the other back into line
through fear and intimidation.
Controllers live in constant
fear of losing their position
of power and authority.

Authoritarians fear opening up and becoming vulnerable. Submissive partners fear being attacked and overwhelmed by their controlling mate. Such attitudes totally block intimacy.

Because the authoritarian acts alone, he (or she) often isolates and alienates himself from his spouse as well as others in the family. Since he isolates himself, his partner is starved of closeness and intimacy.

The controller's life
is regulated by 'rules'.
The more rigid the
rules, the happier
controllers appear.
There is a right way
to do everything – their
way. They know what
is best for everyone in
every situation.

A lack of empathy signals a strong message: 'You do not count. You are insignificant and unworthy.' Such an approach invalidates and discourages the development of the partner's self-esteem.

If, in the name of leadership, a husband totally controls his wife, there may be serious consequences. The continual suppression of her desires will eventually deaden her love for her husband.

A woman needs freedom to operate within her sphere of responsibility. She needs to make decisions and changes when necessary, as well as to receive and enjoy support from a husband who encourages her in her role.

Breaking out of the tenacious grip of a controller isn't easy. But it becomes possible with third-party intervention, since weekly accountability for change is required. But there must be a desire for change in both parties.

The system in which *she* rules has all the drawbacks of the *he*-rules system plus others. All factors in homosexuality may not yet be determined, but a strong mother figure and weak father figure appear to be contributing factors.

Through Christ – change is always possible.

A supportive relationship is based on the concept that marriage partners can work together in an orderly and co-operative manner. This is the Christian ideal.

Supportive partners willingly give up their power to dictate or control the other. Neither demands that their way is the only way to get things done, nor do they insist on unquestioned obedience.

In the supportive relationship the couple functions more like a successful corporation with well-defined objectives and common goals. The couple works together in attaining these goals, recognising that each may have different methods or feelings when striving to reach their goals.

In a supportive
relationship the
husband assumes
responsibility for
certain tasks because
of competence in those
areas. The wife manages
other areas suited to
her capabilities.

Though the husband leads the family, he does not assume the characteristics of a dictator.

A supportive relationship has a more even distribution of power where there is a clear division of responsibility and each partner has a balanced sense of control. *It is a mutually submissive, complementary relationship.*

Both partners
think of themselves
as competent, which
contributes to
self-esteem. Both
think of their partner
as competent, which
contributes to the
other's self-esteem.

The only way to beat the enemy is to team up with your partner to protect your marriage from invasion. Recognise that if problems succeed in dividing you, you both lose.

Supportive leadership

An authoritarian
represses individual
freedom;
a leader encourages
freedom of thought
and action.

An authoritarian
is uncompromising;
a leader is
understanding.

An authoritarian
is unyielding;
a leader is adaptable.

Effective leadership principles

1. In order to look out for the welfare of the family, a family leader must know them. After marriage most men become so wrapped up in career pursuits, that wives no longer receive priority. If a man doesn't know his wife, how can he look out for her welfare?

Leadership principle number two:

A responsible family leader must consult with his partner and keep the channels of communication open and clear.

It is hurtful for one partner to discover that a major decision or purchase has been made without their being consulted.

*A husband should take his
wife into his confidence,
ask her opinions on family
matters and listen attentively
as she presents them.*

He needs his wife's advice,
not just to second his own
ideas and opinions. He needs
to recognise her as a partner
who possesses a respected
grasp of situations that he
may not see or comprehend.

When goals are being determined, it is a good idea to take a weekend away from the children and all responsibilities and spend time alone together over goals and objectives for your life together.

**Leadership principle
number three:**
*A family leader sets a
consistent example.*

A leader needs to set a
consistent example of
godly qualities, which
include integrity, morality
and responsibility.

Leadership principle number four:

The successful family leader oversees family policies and division of tasks and makes sound and timely decisions.

A supportive husband will not make unreasonable demands on his wife but instead be sensitive to the multiple demands on her time and position, just as he expects her to be understanding of his position.

A supportive husband will practise mutual submission, not always giving in to his wife's requests or opinions, but always listening to her with respect and dealing fairly with her.

The making of sound and timely decisions takes much thought, work and prayer. One of the tremendous advantages of putting yourself under God's control is that you have the entire resources of Heaven at your disposal.

God's Word promises that
he will instruct and guide
us in the way we should go.
Making sound decisions
means that the leader will
not only listen to his wife,
but he must then search for
a compromise on each issue
that meets both their needs.

When the couple is caught in an impasse, the family leader must ask, 'What should we do to serve the best interests of the relationship?' not 'What can my partner do to serve my interests?'

The family leader must be open to negotiation and compromise. This includes common problems revolving around spending styles, priorities and the use of time, in-law problems, different parenting styles and sexual problems.

Leadership principle number five:

A family leader recognises his wife's gifts and capabilities and encourages her to utilise them.

Men have no difficulty delegating housekeeping tasks, but may feel intimidated when their wife's talents overlap theirs.

Keep your marriage supportive by communicating. Discuss everything – from everyday events to your dreams for the future.

Leadership principle number six:

A family leader takes responsibility for his mistakes.

A man needs to assume responsibility – not just demand submission! And after assuming responsibility, he must take responsibility for his own actions.

The limits of submission

Submission has its limits.
A woman should not bow to every evil
desire and idea of a depraved man. God
has given every wife a conscience and a
mind of her own to use, and she must
draw the line between what she believes
is morally correct and incorrect according
to the Word of God.

The wife should draw the line according to
the principles found in Galatians 5:19-21.
She has no obligation to obey her husband
when he attempts to lead her into evil
practices.

She must, however, leave all condemnation to the Holy Spirit. When she must say no, she should do so with love and respect.

If she wants to go to church and he doesn't, she should go. But she should leave with the same attitude she might have when going to the supermarket – kiss him goodbye without attempts to make him feel guilty for not attending with her.

A continued attitude of
respect and willingness to
submit to her husband, even
when it goes contrary to a
woman's thinking, allows
God to work matters out.
A woman's submission often
softens a husband's negative
attitude towards Christianity,
for he cannot help respecting
a faith that leads his wife to
give so much of herself to him.